Contents

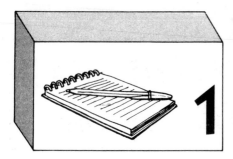

1 Making a Note

Everybody should be able to write in sentences. But sometimes, when we are writing just for ourselves, we don't need to write a complete sentence. A few words are enough to remind us of something we want to remember.

If someone wrote you a letter, asking you for Andy Brown's telephone number, you would write back:

Andy Brown's telephone number is Walton 4156.

But if you had to look up his number for yourself for the first time, you would probably only write:

Andy Brown, Walton 4156.

If you knew only one person called Andy, you would write:

Andy, Walton 4156.

If both of you lived in Walton, you would write:

Andy 4156.

You would write the shortest number of words and numbers that would tell you all you wanted to know.

Noting the Number

You live in Tenforth. You need to ring Sue Handley who also lives in Tenforth at 10 North Lane. Look at the entry in the phone book.

● *Now you need to make a note of the number. What do you write down?*

Handley H, 5 Ascot Rd .... Appleton 2974
Handley J, 6 Ashdale St .... Appleton 3826
Handley M, Moorgarth Wy ..... Tenforth 913
Handley O, 12 Eastfields .... Appleton 3721
Handley S, 10 North La .... Tenforth 816
Handley T, 3 Whitley Cl .... Appleton 2132
Handley T, 112 Glenfield Av ..... Tenforth 731

BASIC SKILLS

English

Paul Groves and Nigel Grimshaw

JOHN MURRAY

Students' Book   ISBN 0 7195 4350 9
Teachers' Resource Book   ISBN 0 7195 4351 7

Acknowledgements
Cartoons by John Erasmus

First published 1988
by John Murray (Publishers) Ltd
50 Albemarle Street, London W1X 4BD

Reprinted 1988, 1992, 1994, 1995, 1997, 1999, 2000, 2002

Printed in Great Britain at
Athenæum Press Ltd, Gateshead, Tyne & Wear

British Library Cataloguing in Publication Data

Groves, Paul
  Basic skills : English.
  Students' book
  1. English language—Grammar—1950–
  I. Title   II. Grimshaw, Nigel
  428   PE1112

ISBN 0-7195-4350-9

Sale Time

You are just going into town. A friend asks you to find out about the one-day sale at the big store, Markham's, next week. He asks you to make a note for him. You are to look in Markham's window and find out on what day the sale will be held, and at what time it starts. This is the notice you see in Markham's window.

- *What do you write down?*

Fun Run

You live in Walton. You would like to join in the local Fun Run which is being held soon. You find this announcement on the noticeboard of your local Leisure Centre.

- *What note do you make so that you can ring the Secretary?*

WALTON FUN RUN

The Walton Circuit Fun Run will take place on Saturday, 13th May, starting from Oakhill Park gates at 11 o'clock and covering a 10 mile course through Bredham and Overton. The entry fee is £1 and over 1,000 applications are expected. If you wish to take part, you should apply early. Forms and a route-map of the course may be obtained from the Organising Secretary, Ms Sharon Wallace, 14, Langley Avenue, Walton. Tel. 3291.

sentences 2 — Looking at Sentences

In letters and other kinds of writing, you need to write in **sentences**. Sentences begin with a **capital letter** and usually end with a **full stop**.

Punctuate the Sentences

- *Write these out correctly.*

    gavin is coming here next week

    meet me outside the bus station

    you can collect the tickets tomorrow

    we shall be on holiday all week

    you'll find the key in the garage

    please tell me when the job's done

Sentences are not notes. Sentences **make complete sense** to anyone who reads them, not just to the person who has written them.

Pick the Sentences

- *How many of these make **complete sense**? Write out those that are complete sentences.*

    The car will pick you up at the end of Brady Lane soon after 12

    I have gone to a disco and will be home fairly late

    Remember to pick up the shoes before 5.30

    At disco and back fairly late

    Geoff Bredham 318

    End of Brady Lane soon after 12

    Geoff's telephone number is Bredham 318

    Shoes before 5.30

- *Have you ended each of the sentences with a full stop? Check!*

6

If a sentence is a question, it ends with a question mark instead of a full stop.

Find the Questions

- *Write out the sentences that are questions. End each one with a question mark.*

I told him about the broken window

Did you find the money

When are you going to see him next

Write to me as soon as you can

How many people were at the meeting

Rodney has got himself a new job

Why was Linda so angry with her mother

Sentences from Notes

Webster's, a television firm, ring you about delivering your new television set. They will bring it tomorrow afternoon at about two o'clock. You want to make sure that someone will be there to let them in. You will be out all day. Your parents are away at the moment, but they will get back tomorrow morning, after you have gone out. You make these notes of your conversation with Webster's.

- *Write a short note to your parents, in complete sentences, explaining what is going to happen. Tell them not to go out, and give them the time when Webster's will be coming.*

Webster's deliver TV tomorrow – 2 o'clock
– Want someone to let them in.

Using the Alphabet 1

Here is the alphabet in capital letters (also called block capitals or block letters):

A B C D E F G H I J K L M N O P Q R S T U V W X Y Z

Here it is in small letters:

a b c d e f g h i j k l m n o p q r s t u v w x y z

- *Write out these letters in alphabetical order:*

  1 E C D B A G F
  2 L H K O J M N I
  3 Q S U T R P
  4 W V Y Z X

- *Now write out these small letters in alphabetical order:*

  1 h e d g f
  2 l j k i m
  3 q p n r o
  4 w t u y x v s

3 Filling in Forms

On the simplest kind of form you just have to fill in your name and address, like this:

Burchester Urban District Council

Library Application Form

Name ..Jane Smith.......................

Address ...2 Western Avenue...........

....Walton SBH7 8WW..................

If the form says, 'Use BLOCK CAPITALS', use capital letters. These are block capitals or capital letters:

A B C D .... X Y Z

So you write your name and address on the form, like this:

JANE SMITH
2 WESTERN AVENUE
WALTON SBH7 8WW

Some forms may ask you to set out the information differently, like this:

Forenames (first names) JANE MARGARET

Surname ...SMITH...........................

Address ...2 WESTERN AVENUE..........

....WALTON...............................

Postcode ...SBH7 8WW....................

Many forms have to be filled in in a way that suits a computer, so they look like this:

Name | | | | | | | | | | | | |

Each letter has to go into a separate box, like this:

Name |J|A|N|E| |S|M|I|T|H| | |

IMMIGRAT

Forms ask for other information besides names and addresses. You may have to think for a moment about what to write down but usually you can put the information in a few words – or even one word.

If you go to a foreign country from Britain you sometimes have to fill in an **immigration form**. This asks you to state your nationality and what country you come from. Jane Smith would fill hers in like this:

IMMIGRATION FORM
All visitors are requested to fill in this form

Forename ....JANE...

Surname ......SMITH..

Nationality ..BRITISH..

Country of origin .GREAT BRITAIN............................

Passport number ..P457 000B...............................

Where issued ..PETERBOROUGH..............................

Try it Out

- *Now fill in Forms A and B, which your teacher will give you.* Use the information given in this section to help you.*

* See page 5 of the Teachers' Resource Book for Forms.

4 More about Sentences

Cleaning Windows

Here are some instructions for cleaning windows. There are five sentences in the paragraph but the capital letters and full stops are missing.

● *Write the paragraph out in sentences.*

you need a bucket of clean water and a leather using the leather, first wash the window with plenty of water next wring the leather out as dry as you can dry the window with the leather finally, when the window is completely dry, a polish with a clean, dry cloth will make it shine

Making a Pot of Tea

Instructions should be clear and lead you on step by step.

● *Put these instructions in the right order. Write each step as a sentence. Remember to begin each sentence with a capital letter and end it with a full stop.*

leave for a few minutes for the tea to brew

put a tea bag into a small teapot

add milk and sugar to taste

pour the tea into a cup

fill the pot with boiling water

Making Custard

Using the following instructions, you can work out how to make a <u>pint</u> of custard.

- *Put them in the correct order so that each step follows clearly from the one before. Make a sentence out of each step.*

put the mixture back into the pan
take <u>enough</u> from a pint of milk to mix the powder to a <u>smooth paste</u>
when the milk is <u>boiling</u>, pour it <u>onto</u> the paste, mixing well
bring to the boil, stirring well all the time, and the custard is ready
put two tablespoons of the custard powder into a basin with a tablespoon of sugar
heat the rest of the milk in a pan

Dictation 1

- First your teacher will read a passage* to you at normal speed. Don't try to write anything down. Just listen to get the <u>sense</u> of what is being read.

- Your teacher will then read the passage slowly, phrase by phrase. Write down what you hear, word for word.

- Finally your teacher will read the passage again straight through. Now you can check what you have written— and make sure you have put in all the punctuation.

- You will be given time after this to read <u>through</u> what you have written and correct any mistakes you have made. Check your spelling!

Checklist

Here are some of the words from the dictation passage. When you check through at the end, make <u>sure</u> that all these words are <u>spelt</u> like this:

blew (what the wind did)   **blue** (the colour)   **hardly**
first   **hungry**   **many**   **eat**   **café**   **clean**   **both**
watch   **four o'clock**   **would**   **pull**

Check your sentences. Have you started with a **capital letter** and ended with a **full stop**? Do you need any **commas**?

* See page 6 of the Teachers' Resource Book.

5 Making Longer Notes

Notes help if you have to learn or remember certain facts. They are useful if you have to pass on information. You might make notes if you have to give a talk or want to remember important points in something you read or hear.

A—Travel Cash

You are going abroad. You want to know where you can change money in the country you are visiting. In a travel book in the library, you find this:

• Read the passage and then **Find the Answers** to the questions. Your answers will show you what kind of notes you could make from the travel book.

> You can change money and cash travellers' cheques at banks and savings banks. These can be found in all towns and most villages. They are open from 8.30 till 12 in the morning, and from 2 until 4 in the afternoon. They are closed all day at weekends and on public holidays. Other places where money can be changed are large railway stations, airports, and border-crossing points. These are open every day and sometimes at night.

Find the Answers—A

1 Name two places in towns and villages where you can change money.
2 When are these places open? (Use figures.)
3 When are these places closed?
4 Where else can you change money?
5 When are these other places open?

When making notes you write down **facts**—places, names, times and so on. You should ask yourself questions that begin with words like: **Who** ...? **When** ...? **Where** ...? **What** ...? **Which** ...? and sometimes, **Why** ...? and **How** ...?

B—Emergency!

Making notes could help you to learn what to do in an emergency.

● *Read this passage:*

The phone can be a great help in emergencies. Bringing help is one of its most important uses.

Most people have heard of 999. But they may not realise that it can call six services: fire, police, ambulance, cave rescue, coastguard and mountain rescue.

Dialling 999 is free. You don't need money or a card.

When you dial 999 the operator will ask which service you need. Keep calm; don't get flustered. It is more important to talk clearly than fast. Say which service you want—or what's happened.

Wait for the service to answer. Then give the number of the phone you are using and say where you are. Then say where help is needed. Give the address or location. In a country area, road numbers (e.g. near the B1366 turning off the A171) are a great help.

Your phone book will tell you about other emergency services, such as those for Gas, Water or Electricity. It is particularly important to phone if you smell gas in the street or in your house.

● *Answer these questions. Use only a few words or just numbers for each one. Your answers will then be in the form of notes about the facts in the passage.*

Find the Answers—B

1 What number should you dial for emergencies?
2 Which six rescue or emergency services can you call on that number?
3 How should you speak to the operator?
4 What number do you give when the emergency services answers?
5 What other information do you give?
6 What other information is useful if you are in a country area?
7 How much does it cost to ring an emergency service?
8 What are the three other services mentioned in the passage apart from the six main emergency services?
9 Where will you find the numbers for these?
10 When should you ring the Gas emergency service?

A group you like is playing at the Salter Hall, Swindon. You want to buy two £6 tickets for Saturday evening, 9th January. The address of the booking office is: Ticket Office, Salter Hall, Wood Way, Swindon SN5 7DG. Follow these steps to write for the tickets.

THE TAX COLLECTORS

SALTER HALL SWINDON
9 JANUARY ★

1   Addresses

When writing a formal or business letter, you put your own address and the date in the top right-hand corner of the page. Then you put the name and address of the person you are writing to on the left-hand side of the page, just below the level of the date on the other side.

Your address goes here. Make a straight line down the page with each new line of writing. Miss a line and put the date with the year.

3 Hill Lane
Granton
Lincs
NG34 5PD

1st March 1988

The title (or name) and address of the person you are writing to. Make a straight line down the page with each new line.

The Manager
Ticket Office
Salter Hall
Wood Way
Swindon
SN5 7DG

If you don't know the name of the person you are writing to you use their title—that is, you address your letter to 'The Manager' or 'The Personnel Officer' etc.

In this kind of letter, you do not have to put commas or full stops in the addresses.

● *Look at the example shown here. On a clean page, write your own address and today's date in the top right-hand corner. Copy the address of the ticket office on the left-hand side.*

2   Starting your Letter

You start a formal letter with 'Dear Sir' or 'Dear Madam' or, if you don't know if you are writing to a man or a woman, 'Dear Sir or Madam'. If you know the person's name, you write 'Dear Mr McLean' or 'Dear Miss Robinson'. If you don't know if a woman is 'Miss' or 'Mrs' you can write 'Ms'. (Many women prefer this anyway.)

Start your letter here with 'Dear Sir' or 'Dear Madam' or with the person's name if you know it.

> 3 Hill Lane
> Granton
> Lincs
> NG34 5PD
>
> 1st March 1988
>
> The Manager
> Ticket Office
> Salter Hall
> Wood Way
> Swindon
> SN5 7DG
>
> Dear Sir or Madam

3   Ending your Letter

If you started your letter with 'Dear Sir' or 'Dear Madam', you end it with 'Yours faithfully', as shown below. If you started your letter with someone's name, you end it by writing 'Yours sincerely'. Finally you sign your name underneath, and write it again in capital letters, to make it clear.

- *On the page you have been using, leave enough space for about six lines of your handwriting, then write 'Yours faithfully' and your name, as shown here.*

'Yours faithfully' if you started with 'Dear Sir' or 'Dear Madam'. 'Yours sincerely' if you started with a name.

> Yours faithfully
> Karen Clifford
> KAREN CLIFFORD

Pages 14 and 15 showed you how to make your own model layout for a formal or business letter.

- *Here is an example of a **complete** formal or business letter. Use it to check your model layout.*

The Willows
Green Lanes
Granton
Lincs
NG34 5PD

5th June 1988

The Manager
Tourist Information Office
Filey
North Yorkshire
SBH12 3LY

Dear Sir or Madam

I am visiting Yorkshire for part of my summer holiday. I expect to come to Filey. Will you please send me any free booklets of information about your town and the surrounding district? I enclose a stamped addressed envelope.

Yours faithfully

Ravi Jaffrey

RAVI JAFFREY

Finish It Off!

- *Finish your model by writing a letter in the space you left to ask for tickets. Give the name of the group of your choice. Say what seats you want. Add that you are enclosing a postal order for £12 and a stamped addressed envelope. Remember to write in complete sentences. Use the model on this page to help you.*

You could plan your letter like this:

1 Name the group and the date of the concert., You could start: 'I would like to book . . . seats for . . .'
2 State the price of the seats. You could start: 'I would like . . .'
3 Mention the postal order and the stamped addressed envelope. You could start: 'I enclose . . .'

- *Check your spelling and remember to start every sentence with a capital letter and finish it with a full stop.*

7 Answering the Telephone

When you answer the telephone, give the caller your phone number, or your name, or the name of the place where you are taking the call. If you aren't at home, this might be your school or college, or the place where you work.

When you take a call for yourself, you *may* decide to make a note of some of the things your caller says. But if you're taking a call for someone else, you should *always* make a note of the caller's name and phone number, and note down his or her message.

If you don't hear the number properly, ask the caller to repeat it. If you don't hear the name properly, ask the caller to spell it out. If any part of the message isn't clear, don't be afraid to ask the caller to repeat it.

If you want to check that you have got everything right, read it back to the caller and ask if it's correct.

Find the Answers

1 When you answer the phone, you should do one of three things. What are they?
2 You are taking a message for another person:
  a Whose name do you note down?
  b Whose phone number do you write down?
  c What else do you note down?
3 a If you haven't heard a caller's number properly, what do you do?
  b If you don't hear a caller's name properly, what do you do?
  c If some details of a caller's message aren't clear, what do you do?
4 How can you check that you have all the details of the call right?

Work It Out!

● *You work in Aston's Bookshop. Your telephone number is 5957. When you answer the phone, you might say one of three things. Write these three things down. List them* ***a***, ***b*** *and* ***c***.

Formal and Business Letters 2

York Holiday

You are thinking of visiting York for a short holiday. You are going to write to the Tourist Information Centre there to ask them to send you a list or booklet of places in York that do bed and breakfast at reasonable prices.

- *Look back at page 16. Write your own address and today's date, and the following name and address (like your model for starting a formal letter):*
The Manager, Tourist Information Centre, De Grey Rooms, Exhibition Square, York, YO1 2HB.

- *Begin your letter with* **Dear Sir or Madam.**

- *Then you could write your letter like this:*

1 Ask for a booklet which lists bed and breakfast places in or near York. You could begin: *'Do you have a booklet that . . .'*
(This is a question so end it with a question mark.)
2 Ask them to send you the booklet and any other information that might help you. You could begin: *'I would be grateful if you could . . .'*
3 You are sending them a large stamped addressed envelope. You could begin the next sentence: *'I enclose . . .'*
4 Now end the letter correctly and sign it.

- *Here are some more letters for your to write. Use your home address, the address given, and today's date. Look at the model layout on page 16 to help you.*

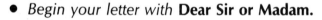

Lost!

The Manager, Lost Property Office, Connor's Bus Services, Marian Way, Nottingham, NG17 4MN.
One day last week you caught a bus at 10 o'clock in the morning from Albury to Nottingham. You left your anorak on the bus. It is light blue and the maker's name inside is *Regatta*.

- *Write to the Lost Property Office. Give all the details of the lost anorak and ask if it has been found.*

Free T-Shirt!

Zestie Crisps Ltd, 57 The Ridings, Havant, Hants, PO7 5NP.

If you send two empty packets of *Zestie* potato crisps and 65p to Zestie Crisps Ltd, they will send you a T-shirt printed with a picture of your favourite sports person, pop star or TV personality.

- *Write to Zestie Crisps. Give the name of the person whose picture you want on the T-shirt and mention that you are enclosing the two packets and a 65p postal order. Because you aren't writing to one particular person, you should begin your letter 'Dear Sirs'.*

Trainers Offer

Special Offer, Springheels Ltd, 17 Broadway, Sutton, Surrey, SM3 4QR.

You have seen some training shoes advertised in a magazine on special offer. The shoes are in red and green, red and grey, blue and grey, or blue and white.

- *Write to the address given and tell the firm your shoe size and the colours you would like. Say that you will send payment when you have tried on the shoes and found them satisfactory. Because you aren't writing to one particular person, begin your letter 'Dear Sirs'.*

Late Delivery

Bardisks Ltd, 114–116 Lastingham Road, Nantwich, Cheshire, CW5 7EF.

About six weeks ago you saw an advertisement in a music magazine and wrote to a firm called Bardisks for a record on special offer. It is called *Dawnflight*, by a group called Tin Soldiers. You sent a postal order for £5·99 with your letter. The advertisement said that you might have to wait 28 days for delivery. You haven't received the record yet.

- *Write to the firm, telling them about your first letter and the money you have sent. Ask them either to send you the record at once or to send you your money back.*

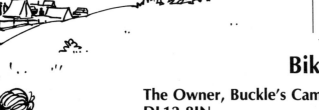

Bike Hire

The Owner, Buckle's Camp Site, Bowes, Co. Durham, DL12 8JN.

You are going camping with your parents in County Durham. You are keen on cycling, and you want to explore the area on holiday, but you can't take your bicycle with you. Your parents have said they will pay for the hire of a bicycle when you get there.

- *Write to the owner of the campsite and ask him or her if it is possible to hire bicycles in the area. If it is, ask for the name and address of the cycle hire firm, so you can write to them. You enclose a stamped addressed envelope.*

9 Taking Telephone Messages

If you are making notes from something written—a notice, a timetable, a book—you can take your time. You can copy words and numbers and check back to the page to see that you have got them right. Making notes of something that is said to you is more difficult.

So you need to listen carefully, and write at the same time. As you know, the things to make notes of are facts and details. When you hear a date, a name, a number and so on, write it down—and go on listening.

Your notes are to help you to remember the message. Don't try to write down everything that is said—there's no time. And there's no need to write in sentences.

But make sure that your notes will make sense to you later. Don't make them *too* short. If someone rings you and says, 'Please tell your sister that Sharma and her friend will be coming next Wednesday', don't just write 'S & f Wed'. You may forget what 'S & f Wed' means by the time you pass on the message. It's better to write something like 'Sharma & friend. Next Wed'.

Find the Answers—A

1 What are the main things to make notes of?
2 What sort of notes should you make?
3 What sort of notes should you *not* make?

Forgetful Fisher

You work in an office for Mr Fisher, who is out at the moment. The phone rings and the caller says:

> Oh, hello, this is Mrs Fisher. I'm afraid my husband has forgotten his tablets and he needs to take a couple during the day. I've just found them on the kitchen table. Will you please tell him that I'm coming to town at about 11. I'll leave them with the receptionist at the main entrance for him to pick up.

- *Read the passage carefully and then **Find the Answers** to the questions. Your answers will show you the sort of notes you should take.*

Find the Answers—B

1 Who is calling? (two words)
2 Who is the message for? (two words)
3 What things are mentioned in the message? (one word)
4 Where were these things found? (Not more than three words)
5 Where can they be picked up? (Not more than four words)
6 At what time can they be picked up? (Not more than three words)

Listen!

You will now hear three short telephone calls. After each, you will be asked questions.*

- *As you listen to each call, make notes that will answer questions like these:*

- **Who is calling?**
- **Who is the message for?**
- **What is it about?**
- **What has to be done?**

_____ Using the Alphabet 2 _____

- *Put this list of names into alphabetical order. (Work it out from the first letter of each name.)*

  Stafford
  Patel
  Wright
  Macintosh
  Hassan
  Anastasi

- *Write down the letters that answer these questions:*

1 What letter comes before H?
2 What letter comes before P?
3 What letter comes after N?
4 What letter comes before E?

- *What word do the four letters spell?*

*See pages 6 and 7 of the Teachers' Resource Book for text and questions for telephone calls.

10 Reading and Remembering

A—Shopping Trip

You are staying with relatives in a town you have never visited before. You have agreed to do some shopping for them. When you get up, you find they have gone out to work, leaving you this note:

Could you please get a bottle of 100 aspirins from Lawson's, the Chemist in the High Street? Here is the bill and the money to pay the TV rental at Hall and Thomson's. Their shop is just across the road from the chemist's. Could you also buy two tins of dog food from Tesco's? Tesco's is on the High Street, too.

Many thanks!

- *Read the note and then* **Find the Answers** *to the questions.*

Find the Answers—A

1 What is the first thing you have to buy?
2 What is the name of the chemist's?
3 In which street will you find it?
4 Where do you pay the TV rental?
5 Where will you find the rental shop?
6 What do you have to get for the dog?
7 Where will you buy that?

B—Warehouse Work

You are in charge of furniture in an office block. These are the instructions for the day:

Put two armchairs in Reception and move the big desk in Reception to the store-room. Take an office chair to room 29 on the second floor, and another to room 34 on the third floor. Take the small grey filing cabinet from the store-room up to Mr Benson's office: room 38 on the third floor.

- *You have a new helper. Read the instructions then* **Find the Answers** *to the questions about what he has to do.*

Find the Answers—B

1 What must he put in Reception?
2 Where must the big desk in Reception go?
3 In which room does an office chair go?
4 Where does another office chair have to be delivered?
5 What has to be taken out of the store-room?
6 Where does that have to be taken?

C—Foreign Students

You are looking after a party of foreign students, all staying with different families. Two of them have to be collected and taken down to the bus station tomorrow. Your helper lives near Mrs Shah and is going to collect the students. She comes round for instructions. This is what you have arranged.

The two students are to be collected from Mrs Shah's house at 4 Lime Grove at about 8.30 a.m. so that they get down to the shopping centre at Wenfield before 9. They will be picked up there at about 9 o'clock by Mr Close. He will be driving a red Fiesta, number A159 RDY. He will take them down to the bus station and make sure that they catch the right bus.

- **Find the Answers** *to check what your helper has to do.*

Find the Answers—C

1 What is Mrs Shah's address?
2 At what time should your helper pick the students up from Mrs Shah's?
3 Where must she take them?
4 At what time will the students be picked up there?
5 What make of car will Mr Close be driving?
6 What is its number?
7 Whose job is it to see that the students get on the right bus?

Here are some more situations where you are given details of things to do.

- *Read the notes and then* **Find the Answers** *to the questions.*

A—Newsagent's Shop

You work for Mrs Slater, who owns a newsagent's shop.
You get in early one morning to find this note from her.

I've got the flu and I can't get into the shop today. I hope to be in tomorrow, if I'm feeling better. Please can you see that Mrs. Desai gets her copy of 'Weekend' today. The paper-boy forgot to deliver it to her last week and she had to come all the way to the shop to pick it up. Tell him to make sure she gets one this week. Crabtree's will be delivering sweets and chocolates during the morning. Sign for them and see that they are stored in the back room. A salesman from Harpin's (the firm that supplies us with pens, pencils, rulers, etc.) will also be calling sometime today. His name is Mr. Dale. Tell him I'm ill and ask him to call again on Friday next week. Many thanks.

Find the Answers—A

1 If someone asks when Mrs Slater will be back, what do you say?
2 What must the paper-boy make sure he delivers to Mrs Desai today?
3 What happened to it last week?
4 What firm will be making a delivery during the morning?
5 Where must you tell them to store the sweets and chocolates?
6 Who else will be calling during the day?
7 What must you ask him to do?

B—Charity Collection

You and a friend have volunteered to do some collecting for a charity. You get these instructions from the organiser on the day before.

> Get the collection boxes and the lapel stickers from Martins' pet shop in Mount Street. Be there early, if you can, and if the shop hasn't opened, go round to the back door. The Martins live over the shop and they have agreed to hand out boxes and flags any time after 7.30 in the morning. Your area is the Clement Estate. Start at the bottom of Pinetree Lane, opposite the Crown and Anchor pub, and work your way up to Elm Avenue. Then go down South Drive and come back up Bonner Road. I'll come round in the evening to pick up the collection boxes and any remaining stickers. I can't give you an exact time but I hope to be at your house between 7 and 8. Can you make sure that there's someone at home to hand the things over to me?

Find the Answers—B

1 Where do you collect your boxes and stickers?
2 What should you do if the shop is closed?
3 From what time in the morning can you collect your boxes and stickers?
4 Where is your collection area?
5 Where do you start?
6 Which road do you go up first?
7 Where do you go next?
8 Up which road do you come back?
9 When will the boxes and stickers be collected from you?
10 What is the last thing the organiser asks you to do?

Dictation 2

- First your teacher will read the passage* to you at normal speed. **Don't try to write anything down.** Just listen to get the sense of what is being read.

- Your teacher will then read the passage slowly, phrase by phrase. Write down what you hear, word for word.

- Finally your teacher will read the passage again straight through. Now you can check what you have written—and make sure you have put in all the punctuation.

- You will be given time after this to read through what you have written and correct any mistakes you have made. Check your spelling!

*See page 6 of the Teachers' Resource Book.

Checklist

Here are some words from the dictation passage. When you check through at the end, make sure that all these words are spelt like this:

**altogether   sure   idea
wrong   everyone
immediately   program
happened   interest**

Have you remembered **capital letters** and **full stops**?
Do you need any **commas**?

12 Forms, Facts and Figures

Some forms ask for more than your name and address. You may be asked for more detailed information, which you will have to think about.

Bike Insurance

You're thinking of buying a motor-scooter. You know the price, and you want to know how much the insurance will cost. You have to fill in a form so that the insurance agent can give you a quotation.

- *Your teacher will give you a form Application for Insurance Quotation.* Use the following information and your own personal details to fill it in.*

Your **Area** is the district in which you live. If you live in a large town, give its name.

The motor-scooter you want to buy is a Yamazuki, model 50. It was built in 1985 and its registration number is B123 MPY. It costs £350.

You can choose from two kinds of insurance policy, **Comprehensive** or **Third Party**. If you have an accident with Third Party insurance, the insurance company will not pay for any damage you do to your own vehicle. But it is cheaper than Comprehensive. Comprehensive insurance insures you against all damage. Choose which kind of insurance you want and then write **Comprehensive** or **Third Party** opposite the word **Cover** on the form.

You are the **Proposer** and your driving licence is a **Provisional** one.

* See page 8 of the Teachers' Resource Book.

Record Request

You want your local radio station to play a request for a relative or a friend whose address you know. You'll have to choose the record—so pick something that you know your relative or friend will like. You'll also have to make up your own short message to go with it. The message could be for a birthday or an anniversary, or it could just be to say hello.

- *Your teacher will give you a **Record Request** form*. Use the following information to fill it in.*

The programme is called **People to People.** It goes out between 7.45 and 8.45 in the mornings, between 3 o'clock and 4.30 in the afternoon, and between 6 and 7 in the evenings, Monday to Friday.

On Saturdays and Sundays the programme goes out in the morning between 9 o'clock and 12.

During the breakfast show from Monday to Friday (7.45 to 8.45) the programme sends out *only* birthday or anniversary greetings. You'll have to remember this if you are *not* sending a birthday or anniversary message. You'll also have to pick a time when you are fairly sure that your friend or relative can be at home to hear your message.

- *Write the message in sentences, **not** in note form.*

Sentence Practice 1

- *Add words of your own to the beginning of each of these to make a sentence, and then write the sentences out.*

.... to go into town to do some shopping.

.... is what I dislike most.

.... round to the back of the house.

.... the whole evening watching television.

.... carefully cleaning her car.

.... when he wrote his poem.

* See page 9 of the Teachers' Resource Book.

13 Formal and Business Letters 3

Look at pages 14–16 to remind yourself how to set out a business letter.

- *Write one or more of these letters, using the model on page 16. Use your own address and today's date.*

BMX

- *Write to **Mr Dale, Ruddle's Farm, Mexwold, Cumbria, CA18 3MD.***

Mr Dale is a farmer and you have heard that he allows BMX riders to use a course on his land. You would like to arrange a BMX meeting at Ruddle's Farm for 9th May. You would like to book the field from 9 am to 4 pm, and you need to know how much Mr Dale would charge. You have heard that the last group of bikers who used the field left a lot of litter, and Mr Dale was annoyed about this. Explain to him that your meeting will be properly run and supervised, and that all litter will be picked up and removed afterwards.

A Day Away

- *Write to **The Booking Office, Dolphin Ltd, 2 Key Street, Hamble, Hants, SO21 7HK.***

You want to take a party across to the Isle of Wight by hydrofoil (a fast boat which rides like a surfboard on top of the water). You would like to make the trip on Friday, 19th June. You want to leave Hamble between 9 and 10 am, and come back between 6 and 7 pm. Ask for a list of departure times between these times. You will be taking about 20 people. Ask if you can book tickets in advance, so that you know there will be room for all of you. What is the normal cost of a ticket? Will they make a reduction for a large party booking in advance? If so, how much?

Computer Show

- *Write to* **The Information Officer, National Exhibition Centre, Birmingham, B3 5AW.**

Starting on the 10th of next month, there is a big three-day computer show in Birmingham. It is not really open to the public, as it is put on for business companies. You and four friends are very interested in computers. You would all like a career in computing. Explain this and ask if you can go to the show. You could offer to pay an entrance fee. Say how much you would be willing to pay.

Going Camping

- *Write to* **Mrs Kirkby, White Horse Farm, Ramwell, Derby, DE4 9RL.**

You have been asked to arrange a camping holiday for a party of 14 people. Mrs Kirkby's site has been recommended to you. You want to make a booking from 9th to 16th July. You will be taking four cars and five tents. Ask her if she can take your party for the dates you need, and what the charge for the week will be. You would want to arrive before midday on 9th July. You have heard that Mrs Kirkby objects to people lighting fires in her field. You might mention that you all have Calor gas stoves, so you would not light any fires.

Charity Disco

- *Write to* **The Manager, The Memorial Hall, Woolby, Bucks, SL3 5LE.**

You are organising a disco for charity at the hall. It is to take place on Saturday, 15th February. You would like to hire the hall from 7 pm until midnight. The disco will start at 7.30 pm and end at 11.30 pm. You would like to know the charge for the evening. You also ask if you will have to pick up and return a key, or if there is a caretaker who will unlock the hall and lock up for you. You also say that you have heard that there has been trouble at the hall from some badly organised discos. Your disco will be properly run and supervised. You would also like the Manager's permission to serve soft drinks and snacks and you want to know if there are facilities for washing up.

Spoken Information

14

You may be asked to go on an errand or to pass on a message. As you know, when listening to spoken instructions, it is sensible to take notes.

Band Time

- *Read the message below. Then* **Find the Answers** *to see what notes you should make.*

A friend of yours plays in a band. The person who runs the band meets you and says, 'When you see Shona, tell her there is a practice in the Hanley Hall at 7 o'clock tonight. We'll be practising the songs for the next gig, so tell her to bring her copy of the lyrics. I expect the practice'll be over between 9 and 9.30.'

Find the Answers

1 Who is the message for?
2 Where will the practice be held?
3 At what time will it be held?
4 What will the band be practising?
5 What should your friend take with her?
6 About what time will the practice finish?

Listen!

You will now *hear* some messages.* You will be asked questions after each message.

- *Make notes as you listen.*

1 Mrs Harris's Message

Your boss, Mr Lee, is late for work this morning. Mrs Harris comes into the office which you share with Mr Lee. Your teacher will read you what Mrs Harris says.

2 Delivering a Newsletter

You have volunteered to deliver some newsletters for a Mrs Marshall. She calls round at your house to tell you what to do. Your teacher will read you what Mrs Marshall says.

*See pages 10 and 11 of the Teachers' Resource Book.

3 Working for Mr Nandra

You have a Saturday job working on a market stall which sells cloth. You work for a Mr Nandra. On Friday night he comes to your house with some instructions. Your teacher will read you Mr Nandra's instructions.

Using the Alphabet 3

Alphabetical Order—the Second Letter

If the first letters of a group of words are all the same, look at the **second letter** to put them into alphabetical order. So

tin	ten	tree	tame	ton	thin

in alphabetical order would be:

tame	ten	thin	tin	ton	tree

following the alphabetical order

a b c d **e** f g **h i** j k l m n **o** p q **r** s t u v w x y z

Work It Out!

● *Put each list of words into alphabetical order:*

1 **fun   frame   fat   fine   foul**
2 **proud   pale   physical   plate   pen   pig   pole**
3 **dead   driver   dune   day   diet   dough**

Speed test!

How quickly can you write down the letter of the alphabet that comes *after* each of these?

f   m   x   t   l   p   j   q   o

How quickly can you write down the letter of the alphabet that comes *before* each of these?

g   v   d   i   r   q   l   z   n

A—Making Caramel

For this recipe you will need five tablespoonsful of sugar and three tablespoonsful of water.

Put the sugar in a pan. Then put the pan on the lowest heat. Keep shaking or stirring the pan until the sugar melts and turns reddish-brown. (Don't let it get dark brown or it will taste bitter.) Take it off the heat as soon as it is reddish-brown and mix in three tablespoonsful of boiling water, stirring in one tablespoonful at a time. (Do this carefully; the boiling water may spit as you add it to the hot sugar.) When the sugar and water are well mixed, put the pan on the heat again. Stir for a moment or two and then take it off the heat. Put the caramel into a heat-resistant container. When it cools it will still be liquid. You can whisk a spoonful into a glass of cold milk with a scoop of ice cream to make a delicious cold drink.

● *Check that you can follow every stage of this recipe by* **Finding the Answers** *to the questions.*

Find the Answers—A

1 How much sugar do you need?
2 How much water do you need?
3 What sort of heat must you put the pan on?
4 What must you do while the sugar is cooking?
5 What colour should the melted sugar be?
6 What will happen if you let it turn dark brown?
7 How should you add the water?
8 What may happen as the water is added to the sugar?
9 When the water and the sugar are well mixed, what do you do?
10 How long do you keep stirring the mixture when you return it to the heat?
11 Into what sort of container should you put the hot caramel?
12 What will the caramel be like when cool?

B—Car Rally

You are a navigator in a car rally. These instructions will help you to be sure of the route on this section. You will not have time to study the instructions or a map while travelling at speed, so you must know the way.

- *Read the instructions and then* **Find the Answers** *to the questions.*

Section A: Woodford to Hallingham

Leave Woodford village by the road to Castleton. Go up this road for three and a half miles and, when you have just passed a sign marked 'To Yargate Farm' on your right-hand side, turn left down a narrow lane, leaving a small wood to your right. About one mile down this lane you come to a crossroads. It isn't signposted but you turn right and, after about two miles, you come to the main Branby/Hallingham road. Turn right again on this road and continue for two miles until you come to Hallingham. The checkpoint in Hallingham is outside the church in the town centre. It is on the main Branby/Hallingham road.

Find the Answers—B

1 Which road do you take out of Woodford?
2 How far along this road do you go?
3 What must you look out for on your right-hand side?
4 What do you do just after you have passed this sign?
5 What landmark is there to check when you make this turn?
6 What do you come to about one mile along this lane?
7 Which way do you turn at this point?
8 How many miles is it along this stretch to the main Branby/Hallingham road?
9 Which way do you turn when you reach this main road?
10 How far then is it into Hallingham?
11 Where is the checkpoint in Hallingham?
12 As you are heading towards the checkpoint, the driver asks you, 'Do we have to turn off this road to get to the church?' What do you answer?

Sometimes you will have to listen to a fairly long talk, giving you important information about things you want to know. It will give you many more details and facts than a telephone call and you will have to take more notes.

Listen!

Imagine that you have just joined a large firm with several other trainees. You are going to hear a talk* explaining what will happen on a trip which is part of your training. Use this talk to practise listening and making notes. Your teacher will read the talk twice. Have rough paper ready for making notes.

Before you listen

Read the questions through to yourself. Write the numbers in a list on your rough paper ready for your notes.

While you listen

If you are a quick reader, keep an eye on the questions while the talk is being read. Make a short note (two or three words) to answer each question. Remember that you make notes mainly about times, places, names and other details. Don't worry if you miss a question or two the first time.

After the first reading

Look through the questions. Have you missed any? If so, answer as many as you can from memory. Then, during the second reading, watch out for the answers to the questions you missed and make notes on these.

After the second reading

You will be given time to write out the answers to the questions, using the notes you have made.

- *Your teacher will now read the talk to you.*

*See pages 11 and 12 of the Teachers' Resource Book.

Questions about the Training Trip talk

1 At what time will the bus leave?
2 Where will it start from?
3 Where is the first pick-up point after that?
4 Where is the second pick-up point?
5 At what time is it expected to reach Mansfield?
6 How will people be taken round the factory?
7 At what time will lunch be served?
8 Where will it be served?
9 What will there be a chance to do before and after lunch?
10 Where will the party travel to after lunch?
11 At the Mansfield factory, where will the bus leave from?
12 At what time will it leave?
13 What are the party asked *not* to do then?
14 At what time will the party arrive at Head Office?
15 In Derby, where will all the party gather for the talks?
16 Who will be giving the talks?
17 What will happen after the talks?
18 At what time will the party leave Derby?
19 Where will the bus stop before it reaches the market-place?
20 At about what time will the party arrive back at the market-place in town?

Dictation 3

- First your teacher will read a passage* to you at normal speed. Don't try to write anything down. Just listen to get the sense of what is being read.

- Your teacher will then read the passage slowly, phrase by phrase. Write down what you hear, word for word.

- Finally your teacher will read the passage again straight through. Now you can check what you have written— and make sure you have put in all the punctuation.

- You will be given time after this to read through what you have written and correct any mistakes you have made. Check your spelling!

*See page 6 of the Teachers' Resource Book.

Checklist

Here are some words from the dictation passage. When you do your final check, make sure that these words are spelt like this:

**frightened   listened   noise
stopped   remembered
neighbours   almost   heard
someone**

Have you remembered **capital letters** and **full stops**? Do you need any **commas**?

Remembering Details

Special Assignment

You are a secret agent. You have microfilm to deliver, and you must make sure you are not followed. It will not be safe to take these instructions with you.

- *Can you remember the instructions? Read them through and then work with a friend. Take turns at asking each other to* **Remember the Answers.** *Who can answer the most questions correctly without looking back at the instructions?*

Take the 9.52 train on Monday morning to Ashertown. Wear a raincoat, glasses and a hat. Carry a brown paper parcel. On arrival in Ashertown, take a number 15 bus to the town centre. Next to the Midland Bank, you will see Woodruff & Banks, an estate agent. At 11.15 precisely, go into the estate agent's and ask for Mr Temple.

The receptionist will direct you into an inner office. When you go in, it will be empty. Leave your hat, coat, glasses and parcel on a chair in this office. Put on the anorak and hat that you will find on the desk. Go out at once by the back door to this office. You will find yourself in a small yard. There will be a bicycle leaning against the wall.

You will find a map in the pocket of the anorak. Use this to make your way by bicycle to Oakhill Park. Go into the park through the Lansdowne Road entrance and take the path towards the lake. On your side of the lake you will see a wooden shelter, painted green. Enter the shelter at 12.15 precisely. A long bench runs all the way along the back of the shelter. At the Lansdowne Road end of this bench, on the floor underneath it, you will find an empty packet of *Hamlet* cigars. When you are sure no one can see you, put the microfilm into this packet and put it back under the bench where you found it.

Using the map, cycle to the station and return to base, leaving the bicycle against the wall outside the station entrance. You will be contacted in the usual way on Monday evening.

Remember the Answers!

1. On what day are you to go to Ashertown?
2. What is the time of the train you must catch?
3. Which three things should you wear?
4. What are you told to carry?
5. What is the number of the bus you must catch in Ashertown?
6. What is the name of the estate agent?
7. At what time must you go into the estate agent's?
8. Who must you ask for there?
9. What must you leave behind in the empty inner office?
10. What clothing must you change into?
11. Where do you have to go after leaving the estate agent's?
12. In which direction should you walk in the park?
13. What will you see near the lake?
14. At what time must you enter this place?
15. What important packet will you find there?
16. What must you put into this packet?
17. Where must you put the packet after that?
18. Where must you go next?
19. When will you receive further instructions?

_____ Sentence Practice 2 _____

- *Add words of your own to each of these to make a sentence and write it out correctly:*

without listening to what I was saying ....
the man in the dark coat ....
because the train was late ....
she did not know that ....
as the old lady was crossing the road ....
he asked me if ....

Don't forget capital letters and full stops!

Replying to Business Letters

No Strings

You work in Franklin's Music Shop and receive the letter shown here.

You check the stock and find that you have no *Melody* or *Black Prince* strings. But you do have a set of *Tower* brand strings, which are of the same quality as the others and the same price. You decide to send these to Ms Wallace.

- *Write the letter that you would send with the set of strings. Use the model on page 16 to help with the layout.*

- *Now choose one of the letters on the opposite page and write a reply. Use today's date, and check the layout with the model on page 16.*

> 3 Hall Place
> Bexhill
> East Sussex
> TN40 7PA
> 5th August 1988
>
> Franklin's Music Shop
> 12 High Street
> Horsham
> Sussex
> RH13 6HT
>
> Dear Sirs
>
> Could you please send me, as soon as possible, a set of 6 strings for an acoustic guitar?
>
> I would prefer a set of 'Melody' or 'Black Prince' but if you do not have either of these in stock, please send me a set of similar price and quality.
>
> I enclose a postal order for £5.00.
>
> Yours faithfully
> Diana Wallace
> DIANA WALLACE

Hotel Booking

You work at the **Norburn Hotel, Wheeldale, Cumbria, LA11 3HW.** You receive a letter from a Mrs Thomson whose address is 5 Ditton Drive, Sale, Cheshire, M33 1XD. She wants to book a double room for herself and her husband for four nights from 4th to 7th July—Thursday, Friday, Saturday and Sunday nights. She would also like to know the cost per night of a double room.

You find that the hotel is full on Thursday, 4th July, but you can book Mr and Mrs Thomson in for the other three nights, Friday, Saturday and Sunday, 5th to 7th July.

- *Write her a letter telling her the position. Say that you charge £65 a night for a double room.*

Country House Visit

You work in the office of *Torrington Hall, Sunderland, Tyne and Wear, SR3 3NF.* It is a big, old country house that is open to the public. You receive a letter from a Miss Ahmad of Ruskin School, Walsall, Staffs, W86 6LX. Miss Ahmad wants to know which months of the year the hall is open, and at what times.

The Hall is open to the public from 1st May to 30th September every year. During that period it is open from 9.30 am to 7.30 pm on Saturdays and Sundays. On Mondays it opens from 9.30 am to 12.30 pm only. It is closed all day on Wednesdays. On Tuesdays, Thursdays and Fridays, it is open from 9.30 am to 5 pm.

- *Set out these times on the form your teacher will give you*. Then write to Miss Ahmad, telling her that you are sending a form with the opening times.*

Guitar Repairs

You are still working at **Franklin's Music Shop, 12 High Street, Horsham, Sussex, RH13 6HT.** You receive a letter from a Mr Anson. He lives at 9 Rose Cottages, Moorham, Sussex, RH11 7MM. A pick-up on his electric guitar has gone wrong. He is writing to ask whether Franklin's repair electric guitars. Your shop doesn't repair musical instruments, but there is a firm in Grantham that does: Electra Ltd, 27/8 Horton Industrial Estate, Grantham, NG32 1DP.

- *Write to Mr Anson, suggesting he gets in touch with the Grantham firm.*

*See page 13 of the Teachers' Resource Book.

19 Memo

Here is another chance to practise following written instructions. You arrive at work to find your boss has left you a **memo** (short for **memorandum**) with these instructions for the day.

- *Read the instructions carefully, then* **Find the Answers.**

MEMO

I'll be going straight to the works tomorrow so I shan't be coming into the office. You can reach me at the works on 45398 until about 12. I shall be with Ms Panayi. Her extension is 54.

During the morning, you'll probably be given the figures for next year's forecast. These will arrive in an office envelope. Take them out of the envelope and check that they are headed 'Forecast for the First Quarter-Year'. Take them to Miss Rodney in Room 212. Explain that I'm out all day and can't look at them. But tell her that I'll want them back tomorrow without fail. This is important. Make sure that she understands that I must have them back first thing in the morning.

You may also get a call from a Mr Denison who works for Sogram Ltd in Nottingham. If you do, take his number, and ring me at once. I'll be in the Main Depot in the afternoon, probably between 2 and 5.30. The number is 45317 and I'll be with the Manager, Mr Hassan. His extension is 72. If Mr Denison rings during the afternoon, ring me at once at the Depot and let me know.

Find the Answers

1. Until what time in the morning will your boss be at the Works?
2. What is the telephone number of the Works?
3. What is the name of the person your boss will be seeing there?
4. What is the number of the extension at which you can reach him?
5. What may you be given during the morning?
6. How will you check that these are the right figures?
7. Where must you take them?
8. What important message must you give to that person?
9. Who may telephone during the day?
10. What must you do if you receive that call?
11. Where will your boss be in the afternoon?
12. Between what times will he be there?
13. What will his number there be?
14. What is the name of the person he will be with?
15. At what extension can he be reached?

Using the Alphabet 4

We use the alphabet to list things in order. Surnames are more important than first names or initials so we list names alphabetically like this:

R K **A**llen
William **B**redon
Andreas **C**hristodoulou
Betty **D**ring

In directories and official lists, the surnames are listed first, like this:

Allen R K
Bredon William
Christodoulou Andreas
Dring Betty

- *List these names in alphabetical order with surnames first:*

H J McDonald
Paula Tate
Peter J Scott
M Gupta
G Vasilou

Julie Lamb
David Rosenberg
H Chan
S Evans

Rashid Ahmad
Q R Williams
Nigel Irving
A O'Toole

Listen!

This is another chance to practise making notes and answering questions. You have just arrived at a hostel at the start of a venture holiday, which involves outdoor sporting activities. The group leader gives a talk about what is going to happen during the holiday.

Before you listen
Read the questions through to yourself. Write the numbers in a list on your rough paper ready for your notes.

While you listen
If you are a quick reader, keep an eye on the questions while the talk is being read. Make a short note (two or three words) to answer each question. Remember that you make notes mainly about times, places, names and other details. Don't worry if you miss a question or two the first time.

After the first reading
Look through the questions. Have you missed any? If so, answer as many as you can from memory. Then, during the second reading, watch out for the answers to the questions you missed and make notes on these.

After the second reading
You will be given time to write out the answers to the questions, using the notes you have made.

● *Your teacher will now read the talk to you.**

Questions about the Venture Centre Talk

1 Where will you go when the talk is over?
2 In addition to wet-weather clothing, what two other things will you be given?
3 What happens if you lose any of this equipment?
4 How many days will you spend fell-walking?

*See page 14 of the Teachers' Resource Book.

5 Who will go on these fell-walking trips?
6 At what time do they start?
7 When are they expected to finish?
8 What sort of route will they take?
9 What other activities will you try?
10 How many groups will you split up into for these?
11 How many groups will do canoeing at one time?
12 How many will do climbing?
13 What games can be played in the Centre in the evenings?
14 What can people do if they don't want to play games?
15 What is going to happen on your last night?
16 At what time is the evening meal?
17 Between what times is breakfast served?

Sort It Out!

This is one person's description of the venture holiday you have just heard about. The sentences in the description have got into the wrong order and have lost their punctuation.

on the last night we had a disco which was really great

for our first supper we had hamburgers, peas and chips and ice cream

I liked the canoeing best—even though it rained

I was very pleased when I heard we were going on a venture holiday

after Barry's talk we went and collected our stuff from the store and then we had supper

on the first morning they split us up into two groups

we had some good laughs in the coach on the way to the Centre

the first thing that happened when we got to the Centre was a talk from Barry about the plans for the holiday

my group did canoeing first, then on the second day we did climbing practice

we were all very sorry to come home

it was raining on the third day, too, when we went fell walking

- *Write down the continuous description when you have sorted out the order of the sentences. (Don't forget the capital letters and full stops!)*

Filling in an Application Form

- *Suppose these firms were within reach of where you live. Pick the job you would like best. Then fill in the application form, which your teacher will give you.**

Young person wanted for clerical duties. Good prospects for someone willing to learn. Apply to Miss F. Adam, Benson and Wall, Estate Agents and Auctioneers, Kingsland House, Kingsland Court, Webberley VW2 4SF

Trainee Storekeeper wanted for car firm. Tidy and efficient. Apply Marland Garages Ltd, Wanford Avenue, Villerby XT3 9QR

Person wanted to train for furniture assembly. Write to the Managing Director, Mobelart Ltd, 19 King Street, Stenton-on-Trent, FR16 4WP

Trainee Hairdresser required. Apply Tonio's, 27 High Street, Mockerby QS3 4WX

Window Dresser wanted for go-ahead Department store. Training given but must be really interested in the job and be willing to work at evenings and weekends. Apply to Marketing Manager, Dart and Ford, Castle Street, Barchester, TD3 U4

Trainee machine Operator required. Shift work. Apply Dexadren Plastic Ltd, 40 Industrial Estate, Drybarton, GH4 7DP

Trainee wanted for dairy work. Write to The Manager, Castle Dairy Products Ltd, Warren Court, Blandon SR12 5BW

Young person wanted for Packing Dept. Write to Dispatch Manager, Paraglide Ltd, 27 Industrial Estate, Charlton BS3 2FY

Assistant wanted in shop. Must be fashion conscious and stylish dresser. Apply Suzi's Boutique, Farrell Street, Gadford MO6 9FE

Young Sales Representative for toys, novelties, etc. Must be willing to travel. Jamal Novelties, 15 Foreman Road, Dabbenham TZ15 2RP

Young person wanted to help with horses. Able to ride or willing to learn. Apply Rudd's Stables, Moor Lane, Lower Axford, TB2 8RS

Trainee Labourer wanted for building site. Apply J. Hills, Builder, 4 Harding Road, Metford CD2 1SF

*See page 15 of the Teachers' Resource Book.

Applying by Letter

Harper's is a large stationery, book and music shop in Leicester. They advertised for a trainee shop assistant. Tracey Walters applied.

- *Look carefully at the letter she wrote.*

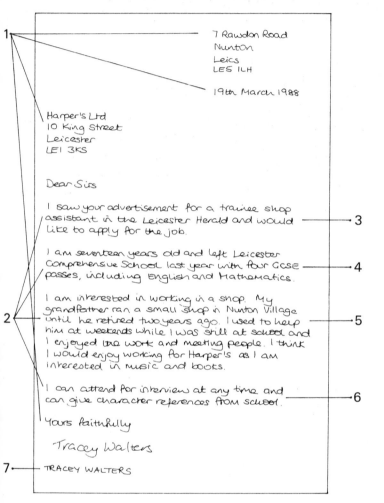

Letter:

1 →

7 Rawdon Road
Nunton
Leics
LE5 1LH

19th March 1988

Harper's Ltd
10 King Street
Leicester
LE1 3KS

Dear Sirs

I saw your advertisement for a trainee shop assistant in the Leicester Herald and would like to apply for the job. — 3

I am seventeen years old and left Leicester Comprehensive School last year with four GCSE passes, including English and Mathematics. — 4

I am interested in working in a shop. My grandfather ran a small shop in Nunton Village until he retired two years ago. I used to help him at weekends while I was still at school and I enjoyed the work and meeting people. I think I would enjoy working for Harper's as I am interested in music and books. — 5

I can attend for interview at any time and can give character references from school. — 6

Yours faithfully

Tracey Walters

7 — TRACEY WALTERS

Try It Out!

- *Pick another job you would like from the ads on page 44. Apply for it by letter. Make sure that you have covered the seven points in the **Checklist**. If you haven't had any work experience, you could mention your hobbies or interests.*

Checklist

1 The letter is set out as a formal or business letter. It gives Tracey's address and the address of the firm she is writing to.
2 It is divided into paragraphs. Each new idea is put into a new paragraph.
3 It mentions the job Tracey is applying for and where she saw it advertised.
4 It gives her age and details of her education and qualifications.
5 It tells Harper's what work experience she has had, and why she might be suitable for the job.
6 It says when she will be free for interview and offers to supply references.
7 Her name is printed clearly under her signature.

22 Setting out Information

You are asked for information about yourself on applications forms and at interviews. Taking time to set it all down is useful. Once you have done it, you can refer to it to fill in application forms or to prepare for an interview. Doing it may help you to remember details about yourself you might otherwise forget. We have set out the example here in the form of a complete self-profile. This is sometimes known as a **curriculum vitae** (or **cv**):

● *Use this as a pattern to set out your own personal details. If you have no information to put under one of the headings, miss that out.*

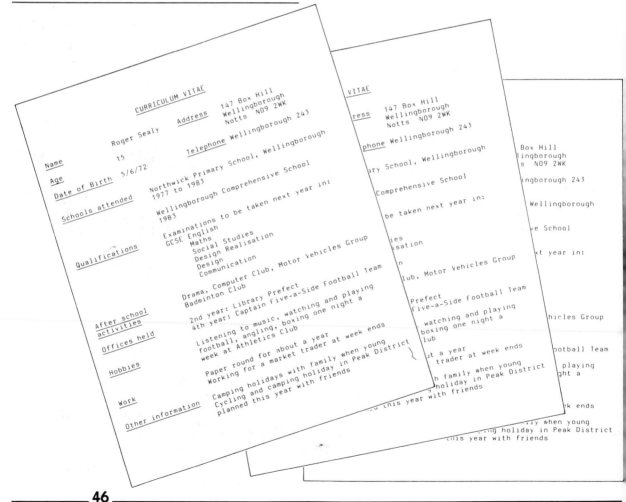

CURRICULUM VITAE

Name   Roger Sealy   Address   147 Box Hill
                                          Wellingborough
                                          Notts NO9 2WK

Age   15   Telephone Wellingborough 243

Date of Birth 5/6/72

Schools attended   Northwick Primary School, Wellingborough
                   1977 to 1983
                   Wellingborough Comprehensive School
                   1983

Qualifications   Examinations to be taken next year in:
                   GCSE English
                        Maths
                        Social Studies
                        Design Realisation
                        Design
                        Communication

After school   Drama, Computer Club, Motor Vehicles Group
activities   Badminton Club

Offices held   2nd year: Library Prefect
                   4th year: Captain Five-a-Side Football Team

Hobbies   Listening to music, watching and playing
                   football, angling, boxing one night a
                   week at Athletics Club

Work   Paper round for about a year
                   Working for a market trader at week ends

Other information Camping holidays with family when young
                   Cycling and camping holiday in Peak District
                   planned this year with friends

Tabulating Information

Setting out information in the form of a table sometimes has an advantage. The details can be seen clearly and at a glance. Compare these two ways of giving information.

A A 70 miles per hour speed limit is in operation on all motorways and urban dual carriageways and a 60 miles per hour limit operates on all other unrestricted roads. In most restricted areas, the speed limit is usually 30 miles per hour.

B

SPEED LIMITS IN MPH (Miles Per Hour)	
Motorways	70
Urban dual carriageways	70
Other unrestricted roads	60
Most restricted roads	30

Stopping Distances

- *Using the table you will be given,* fill it in with this information.*

At a speed of 20 miles per hour, the stopping distance is 40 feet.
At 30 miles per hour, the stopping distance is 75 feet.
At 40 miles per hour, the stopping distance is 120 feet.
At 50 miles per hour, the stopping distance is 175 feet.
At 60 miles per hour, the stopping distance is 240 feet.
At 70 miles per hour, the stopping distance is 315 feet.

*See page 16 of the Teachers' Resource Book.

Accidents

- *Using the table you will be given, fill it in with this information.*

During this time there was a total of 59 accidents to children. 27 were injured by accidents in the home and 32 were injured in traffic accidents. The total number of accidents to adults was 72. 10 adults were injured at home, 25 had accidents at work and 37 were hurt in traffic accidents.

Test Paper 1
Part 1
Listening

Listen and follow while your teacher reads these instructions*:

This test has a practice section and three others. In the practice section and Section A, you will listen to the short messages described in your textbook. After you have listened to each message, I will read the questions. You then write the answers. Each message and its questions will be read **once** only. The first message and questions are for practice and will **not** be marked.

Make notes while you are listening if it will help. Your notes will not be marked. Answer **all** the questions. In your answers, write words and numbers as clearly as you can. You are not allowed to use a dictionary.

SECTION A

1 Telephone Call
You work in an office. The telephone rings. You answer and hear the following message.
(*Your teacher will now read the message and the questions to you.*)

2 Supermarket
You started work in a supermarket a few days ago. Your main job is to see that the shelves are filled with the right goods. One morning the manageress gives you these instructions.
(*Your teacher will now read the instructions and the questions to you.*)

3 Flight to Marbella
You are going on a fortnight's holiday to Marbella in Spain. When you get to the airport, you are told that the flight has been delayed. Then you hear this announcement over the public address system.
(*Your teacher will now read the announcement and the questions to you.*)

*See pages 17–21 of the Teachers' Resource Book.

SECTION B

Listen and follow while your teacher reads these instructions:

In this section you will be read a talk, which is longer than the messages you have just heard. This time you will have to read the questions for yourself, but the talk will be read twice. First you will have a minute to read the questions through to yourself. Then the talk will be read for the first time. Next, you have a minute to re-read the questions and then the talk will be read again. When the second reading is over, you will have four minutes to finish answering the questions.

The talk was given to members of a club who are interested in pop music. The speaker is a musician.
(*Your teacher will now read the talk to you.*)

Questions

1 Where did the speaker first become interested in drumming? *(1 mark)*
2 How many concerts does he say he played in at school? *(1 mark)*
3 How old was he when he bought his first drum kit? *(1 mark)*
4 When was it bought for him? *(1 mark)*
5 Was it a new drum kit? *(1 mark)*
6 Where did he practise on it? *(1 mark)*
7 How did he practise? *(1 mark)*
8 When he first started to practise in this way, what did he do? *(1 mark)*
9 What did he do when he got better at drumming? *(1 mark)*
10 When did he join two other people in a pop group? *(1 mark)*
11 What two instruments did those two play? *(2 marks)*
12 Where did they practise? *(1 mark)*
13 What kind of music did they play? *(1 mark)*
14 What did they hope they were going to do? *(1 mark)*
15 What happened to the group in the end? *(1 mark)*

SECTION C

This is a dictation.* You will be told what you have to do. Do not write anything down until you are asked to do so.

(15 marks)

* See pages 20–21 of the Teachers' Resource Book.

Test Paper 1

Part 2

Reading and Writing

(Time allowed: 1 hour)

SECTION A

Charity Shop

You have agreed to open up and look after a charity shop for the first part of a Saturday morning. The organiser has left you the following instructions. Read them carefully and then answer the questions 1–15 to show that you have understood the instructions.

I have left the keys with Mrs Rajah at 9 Harley Lane. Pick them up from her and try to get to the shop by 8.45 am. As soon as you get in, switch on the heating. You will need money for the till. This money—the 'float'—is in a black cash box. Go upstairs and in the store-room you will see a big wooden desk. The top left-hand drawer of this is locked but you will find the key, with a plastic tag marked 'Desk', on the key ring. Unlock the drawer and you will find the cash box inside. Put the money from this into the drawers of the till. You will need to unlock the till with the smallest key on the key ring.

In the cash box, all the different coins and notes are sorted out into small plastic bags. Empty each of these into a different drawer in the till so that all the different coins are kept separate.

Open the shop at 9 o'clock. All the items on sale have labels stuck to them showing the price. You will be on your own until 9.30 and will have to deal with any customers who come in. At 9.30, Miss Walsh and Mrs Turner should arrive. Miss Walsh will take over the selling from you and Mrs Turner will take you up to the store-room. Then, unless things get very busy in the shop and you are wanted to help out down there, you can spend the rest of the morning with Mrs Turner in the store-room, sorting out and labelling all the items there which have been given to us.

Now answer these questions

1	Where does Mrs Rajah live?	(1 mark)
2	At what time should you get to the shop?	(1 mark)
3	What should you do as soon as you get to the shop?	(1 mark)
4	In what kind of box is the money for the till (the 'float') kept?	(1 mark)
5	Where is the big wooden desk?	(1 mark)
6	In which drawer of this desk is the box?	(1 mark)
7	How is the key for this drawer marked?	(1 mark)
8	Which key unlocks the till?	(1 mark)
9	How are the different coins and notes sorted out in this box?	(1 mark)
10	How do you fill the drawers in the till?	(1 mark)
11	At what time must you open the shop?	(1 mark)
12	Where are the prices for the items on sale?	(1 mark)
13	Which two people should be arriving at about 9.30?	(1 mark)
14	Which of them will take over the selling?	(1 mark)
15	Where will you go then?	(1 mark)

SECTION B

Here is a list of authors. Working by surname only, write them out in alphabetical order.

Bill Naughton
Robert Cormier
Alan Garner
John Wyndham
Susan Hill
Stan Barstow
Bill Forsyth
Chinua Achebe
Roald Dahl
Rukshana Smith
George Orwell
Jan Mark
Laurie Lee
Keith Waterhouse

SECTION C

You will be given a form* to fill in for this section. Read the passage below and then use the details given to help you to fill in the form.

> You have just bought a moped. It is a Sato 50 (50 cc). You bought it last Saturday, so the date you will need for question number 7 is last Saturday's date. The registration number is C169 LPY and its taxation class is 'moped'. You want to get it licensed for 12 months from the first of this month.

(15 marks)

SECTION D

You and your family have picked a village in Greece for your holiday in the sun. Now you have to decide which kind of accommodation in the village would suit you all. Read the following descriptions, pick the most suitable place—the studios, the guesthouse or the hotel— and write a letter to the travel company booking your holiday. Their address is: Sunways Travel, 38 Ash Street, London WC2E 5JS.

APOLLO STUDIOS
These are situated in the centre of the village near the beach and close to bars and restaurants. No meals are provided, but there are basic cooking facilities.

MILOS GUESTHOUSE
This is situated in a quiet stretch of farmland about 2 miles from the village and beach. A bus runs to and from the village every hour until 9 at night. Breakfast and an evening meal are served.

HOTEL GRECO
Situated in the village, the hotel looks out onto the beach. Breakfast, lunch and an evening meal are served. Windsurfers and paddle-boats can be hired from the hotel, which has a swimming pool, and there is a disco every night.

You will need to mention:

(**a**) Which place—the studios, the guesthouse or the hotel—you have chosen;
(**b**) Which fortnight of the summer you want to book for;
(**c**) How many people are going;
(**d**) How many single rooms and how many double rooms you want.

(20 marks)

---

* See page 22 of the Teachers' Resource Book.

Test Paper 2
Part 1
Listening

Listen and follow while your teacher reads you these instructions*:

This test has a practice section and three others. In the practice section and Section A, you will listen to the short messages described in your textbook. After you have listened to each message, I will read the questions. You then write the answers. Each message and its questions will be read **once** only. The first message and questions are for practice and will **not** be marked.

Make notes while you are listening if it will help. Your notes will not be marked. Answer all the questions. In your answers, write words and numbers as clearly as you can. You are not allowed to use a dictionary.

SECTION A

1 Telephone Call
You work in an office. The telephone rings. You answer and hear the following message.
(*Your teacher will now read the message and the questions to you.*)

2 College Interview
You hope to begin a course at Morton College. You receive a telephone call giving you instructions about an interview.
(*Your teacher will now read the instructions and the questions to you.*)

3 Meals on Wheels
You are helping with the meals on wheels service for old people. The organiser gives you these instructions.
(*Your teacher will now read the instructions and the questions to you.*)

*See pages 23–27 of the Teachers' Resource Book.

SECTION B

Listen and follow while your teacher reads these instructions:

In this section you will be read a talk, which is longer than the messages you have just heard. This time you will have to read the questions for yourself, but the talk will be read twice. First you will have a minute to read the questions through to yourself. Then the talk will be read for the first time. Next, you have a minute to re-read the questions and then the talk will be read again. When the second reading is over, you will have four minutes to finish answering the questions.

The talk was given by a person running a small window cleaning service. This part of the talk describes how the business started.

(*Your teacher will now read the talk to you.*)

Questions

1	Why were house windows in Felton so dirty?	(*1 mark*)
2	Whose windows did the person giving the talk clean first?	(*1 mark*)
3	Who was the second person who had windows cleaned?	(*1 mark*)
4	How much was the window cleaner paid for that job?	(*1 mark*)
5	How did the person find out if other people wanted their windows cleaned?	(*1 mark*)
6	How many customers were found in this way?	(*1 mark*)
7	What equipment was bought for the job?	(*1 mark*)
8	What equipment could not be bought?	(*1 mark*)
9	How did the window cleaner solve that problem?	(*1 mark*)
10	What did the window cleaner find tiring during the very early days of the job?	(*1 mark*)
11	What was done to solve this problem?	(*1 mark*)
12	Who helped out with a better means of transport?	(*1 mark*)
13	How did some of the speaker's friends react to this new transport?	(*1 mark*)
14	Who gave the speaker some good advice about price-fixing?	(*1 mark*)
15	What was the hourly rate of pay on which prices were fixed?	(*1 mark*)

SECTION C

This is a dictation.* You will be told what you have to do. Do not write anything down until you are asked to do so.

(*15 marks*)

*See pages 26–27 of the Teachers' Resource Book.

Test Paper 2

Part 2

Reading and Writing

(Time allowed: 1 hour)

SECTION A

Working in a Café

You are interested in a job as an assistant in a café. Here is part of the job description. Read it carefully then answer the questions.

Shifts begin half an hour before the café opens. Staff are expected to arrive punctually for their shift.

Staff are expected to maintain a high standard of personal cleanliness, taking particular care of hands and fingernails. All staff are issued with two work-coats, one of which can be handed in for cleaning at any time. Work-coats should be kept clean and changed as soon as they show any signs of wear.

Serving staff are also responsible for plates and cutlery. The first job when coming on or going off shift is to check that the washing-up machine is empty and ready for use. If any plates or other crockery are found in the machine at the beginning of a shift, staff should report this to Mrs Wilson, the manageress. Any dirty crockery found in the washing-up machine should, of course, be left there. Any clean crockery found in the machine should be stacked in the right place on the shelves.

At the beginning or end of a shift, staff must make sure that all table tops are clean and that the floor has been swept. If staff find that the table tops are dirty or the floor has not been swept, they should clean up and report this to Mrs Wilson. At the beginning of each shift, staff should check that all tables are supplied with salt and pepper, a sugar dispenser and a menu card. Knives, forks and other cutlery are kept in trays behind the counter. Staff should prepare cutlery for customers by wrapping it. A knife, a fork and a spoon should be neatly wrapped in a green paper napkin. These are also kept in boxes behind the counter.

Now answer these questions

1 How soon before the café opens should you arrive to begin your shift? *(1 mark)*
2 What high standard are you expected to maintain? *(1 mark)*
3 What should you take particular care of? *(1 mark)*
4 What are all staff issued with? *(1 mark)*
5 When should you change these? *(1 mark)*
6 What is your first job when coming on or going off shift? *(1 mark)*
7 What should you do if you find crockery in the washing-up machine? *(1 mark)*
8 What should you do if there is dirty crockery in the washing-up machine? *(1 mark)*
9 What should you do with clean crockery you find in the machine? *(1 mark)*
10 Apart from reporting it, what should you do if you find the floor unswept when you come on shift? *(1 mark)*
11 What other area should you check for cleanliness when you come on shift? *(1 mark)*
12 Name two things that should be put out on the tables. *(1 mark)*
13 Where are the knives, forks and spoons kept? *(1 mark)*
14 How do you prepare cutlery for customers? *(1 mark)*
15 Where will you find the paper napkins? *(1 mark)*

SECTION B

Here is a list of magazines. Put them in alphabetical order.

She
Honey
Yachting Today
Woman
Motor Cycling
Gardening World
Over 21
Autocar
Car
Peace News

SECTION C

You will be given a form* to fill in for this section. Read the passage on page 57 and use the details given to help you to fill in the form.

*See page 28 of the Teachers' Resource Book.

While you were on holiday, you went swimming and left a camera and wristwatch on some rocks. They were either washed away by a high wave, or knocked into the sea by a passer-by. You recovered them but the sea water seems to have damaged them beyond repair. Your insurance policy is number 18/1210/8026.

You report the accident to the insurance company, and they send you a form to complete. The camera was a Sektor reflex, worth about £80, and the watch was a Honshu digital, worth about £12.

(*15 marks*)

SECTION D

You have the job of inviting speakers to your school or college. You have heard that your own favourite personality in entertainment or sport is in the country. ('Entertainment' includes films, television, books, pop music and so on.) He or she is very willing to give talks to the public, including schools and colleges.

Write a letter inviting him or her to come to your school or college. You can pay travelling expenses and a fee of £50.

When you write the letter you will need to mention:

(**a**) Why you became interested in him or her, and why you think other people will be interested;
(**b**) The kind of audience he or she will be talking to and the average age of the group;
(**c**) The town, the whereabouts of the school or college, and the day, date and time of day when you would like the talk to take place;
(**d**) The suggested subject of the talk (his or her childhood, how he or she started on a career, his or her achievements or any other subject of your choice);
(**e**) The travelling expenses and fee you can pay.

(*20 marks*)

Test Paper 3

Part 1

Listening

Listen and follow while your teacher reads these instructions*:

This test has a practice section and three others. In the practice section and Section A, you will listen to the short messages described in your textbook. After you have listened to each message, I will read the questions. You then write the answers. Each message and its questions will be read **once** only. The first message and questions are for practice and will **not** be marked.

Make notes while you are listening if it will help. Your notes will not be marked. Answer all the questions. In your answers, write words and numbers as clearly as you can. You are not allowed to use a dictionary.

SECTION A

1   Telephone Call
You work in an office. The phone rings and you take the following message.
(*Your teacher will now read the message and the questions to you.*)

2   Sports Equipment
You are in charge of sports equipment at a club. The organiser gives you the following instructions.
(*Your teacher will now read the instructions and the questions to you.*)

3   Local Radio
You are a secretary of a swimming club. You hear this announcement over the radio. You think the members will be interested and you want the details.
(*Your teacher will now read the announcement and the questions to you.*)

* See pages 29–33 of the Teachers' Resource Book.

SECTION B

Listen and follow while your teacher reads these instructions:

In this section you will be read a talk, which is longer than the messages you have just heard. This time you will have to read the questions for yourself, but the talk will be read twice. First you will have a minute to read the questions through to yourself. Then the talk will be read for the first time. Next, you have a minute to re-read the questions and then the talk will be read again. When the second reading is over, you will have four minutes to finish answering the questions.

The talk is given by a member of the Leisure Centre staff who wishes to publicise opportunities for sport in the area.
(*Your teacher will now read the talk to you.*)

Questions

1   If you can't swim, where can you learn? *(1 mark)*
2   Name a group activity you can take part in at the pool. *(1 mark)*
3   Apart from basketball, what two other court games can you play at the sports centre? *(1 mark)*
4   What can you do if you don't have the equipment to play these games? *(1 mark)*
5   On which night is the coaching class for badminton? *(1 mark)*
6   What is mentioned as well as yoga and keep-fit classes? *(1 mark)*
7   Which two kinds of 'martial arts' are mentioned? *(1 mark)*
8   On which day of the week does the weight-lifting group meet? *(1 mark)*
9   Which activity is mentioned as well as circuit-training? *(1 mark)*
10   What will you find out at Shadwell? *(1 mark)*
11   Apart from dinghy-sailing and wind-surfing, what else can you do on the artificial lake there? *(1 mark)*
12   On which day of the week are all these activities free? *(1 mark)*
13   To which sort of people are the free activities offered? *(1 mark)*
14   What must you wear while taking part in these activities? *(1 mark)*
15   Who will help you to take up the water sports safely? *(1 mark)*

SECTION C

This is a dictation.* Do not write anything until you are told to do so.
(15 marks)

*See pages 32–33 of the Teachers' Resource Book.

Test Paper 3

Part 2

Reading and Writing

(Time allowed: 1 hour)

SECTION A

Helping with a play

You have been asked to help at the performance of a play at your local community centre. The organisers have written the following instructions for all the helpers. Read the instructions carefully and then answer questions 1–14.

The play runs for four evenings. People who do car park duty will not want to be out in the cold all the time. So we will switch the jobs round from evening to evening.

We shall need four people on car park duty. Their job is to make sure that no large spaces are left between parked cars so that we can get everybody in. It would be advisabie for at least one person to remain on duty in the car park until the show is over. Please remind drivers to lock their cars.

At the two entrances to the hall we shall need four people, two just inside each door. We suggest that one of them checks tickets while the other sells programmes and tickets for those who have not already got them. If there is a sudden rush of people at the entrance, both should concentrate on admitting people and stop selling programmes, as these will be on sale in the hall anyway.

Inside the hall the other four people will act as ushers— helping the audience to find their seats. Each of these four should also have a batch of programmes to sell. All programme and ticket sellers can collect programmes, tickets and money for change from Mrs Chambers who will be on duty in the main office. All unsold programmes, tickets and money should be handed in to her when the show is over.

If you want to see the show, please sit or stand at the back of the hall. Then, as soon as the interval starts, please go quickly to the entrance area to help with the serving of refreshments.

Now answer these questions

1. How long will the play run for? (1 mark)
2. Why is it a good idea to switch the jobs round from evening to evening? (1 mark)
3. How many people will be needed for car park duty? (1 mark)
4. What should they make sure of while supervising the parking? (1 mark)
5. What should car owners be reminded to do? (1 mark)
6. How will the four people at the entrances be split up? (1 mark)
7. What will each one's job be? (1 mark)
8. If there is a sudden rush of people waiting to get in, what should be done about programmes? (1 mark)
9. How many people will there be in the hall showing people to their seats? (1 mark)
10. What should each of these people have? (1 mark)
11. Who has the tickets, programmes and change? (1 mark)
12. Where can that person be found? (1 mark)
13. What should happen to programmes, money and tickets when the show is over? (1 mark)
14. Where are those who want to see the show asked to sit or stand? (1 mark)

SECTION B

You work for a doctor. She has been using these people's medical record cards. Put the names in alphabetical order, ready for filing.

Mr T. Williams
Mrs P. Samuel
Mr A. Ladha
Mr R. Richards
Mrs S. Penstone
Mrs J. Porter
Mr N. Lincoln
Mr F. Wilson
Mr N. Desai
Mr A. Hussein
Miss M. McTaggart

(5 marks)

SECTION C

You will be given a form* to fill in for this section. Read the passage below and then use the details given to help you to fill in the form.

A firm which sells a product you like and use often is running a competition. The product could be a snack, such as crisps or chocolate bars, or any item of food, such as breakfast flakes or baked beans. It could be a brand of soap or toothpaste. It could even be a product connected with a hobby of yours, such as an item of sports gear. Think of something you enjoy eating or using and often buy.

You have to fill in a form for the competition, naming the shop where you usually buy the product, and saying in a few words why you find the product so attractive.

(15 marks)

SECTION D

You live in a flat and you have just received a bill from a builder. He has built you a small wooden wardrobe and fixed it to the wall in a corner of your bedroom. The work was done last week.

You are not going to pay the bill because the door of the wardrobe will not close properly, and the back of the wardrobe is starting to come away from the wall.

Write a letter to the builder, telling him you are not going to pay, and why.

You will need to mention:

(a) The fact that you have just got his bill, but are not going to pay.
(b) What the job was, and when it was completed.
(c) What has happened to the wardrobe.
(d) What you think the builder should do about the bad work-manship, and when you would like him to do it.

(20 marks)

*See page 34 of the Teachers' Resource Book.